THE GHOST
of
DYLAN THOMAS

RUTHVEN TODD

Happen*Stance*

ISBN 978-1-910131-00-8

Acknowledgements
Thanks to Christopher Todd, Ruthven's son, for support
and encouragement and to the National Library of
Scotland for permission to reprint from the manuscript in
this edition.

Peter Main, Ruthven's biographer, assisted in far more
ways than are immediately evident. He also supplied the
prefatory photograph of Ruthven wearing what must be
the hat he himself describes on page 4. (Publication of
Todd's biography is planned for 2015.)

Pages 3-19 are an unpublished article by Ruthven Todd
held in the National Library of Scotland titled 'A Good
Quiet Weekend', MS 26857.

Pages 20-27 are extracted from an article edited by Robert
Latona in *The Malahat Review*, No. 62 (1982), pp. 8-60,
titled 'Ruthven Todd, Memoirs'. The section incorporated
here was originally subtitled 'A Different Dylan'. It is
drawn from Todd's unpublished memoir of Dylan Thomas
held in the National Library of Scotland.

Printed by The Dolphin Press
(www.dolphinpress.co.uk)
Published by Happen*Stance*
21 Hatton Green, Glenrothes,
Fife KY7 4SD
www.happenstancepress.com
Further info: nell@happenstancepress.com

THE GHOST
OF
DYLAN THOMAS

THE GHOST OF DYLAN THOMAS

FOR NEARLY FIFTEEN years I was plagued by 'the Dylan Thomas Legend', or rather mess of legends, and of lies. For many of these years I found it difficult to visit a bar in Greenwich village or a pub in Soho without overhearing the rantings of people who had been his 'best friend'. I rather doubt whether Dylan himself would have recognised even ten per cent of these 'friends'.

There was, too, the vulgarity of a play[1] where Katherine Anne Porter allowed herself to be used in a way which was beyond all fantasy, carried around on the shoulders of Alec Guinness, who was playing good Alec Guinness, but with no resemblance to the little Welshman I knew called Dylan Thomas. I was witness to the original event, and all that Dylan did was, rather puffingly, hoist Miss Porter toward the ceiling. He gave a gasp of relief when he lowered her to the floor with no bones broken on either side.

The outpourings have begun to slow to a trickle and few people now dine out on once having got drunk with Dylan. It may still be hard to look upon him coldly, but some degree of objectivity can be reached.

I want to recall a snatch of days which might upset the legend but which were a part of him just as much as another part was represented by the roistering boy. Before I start, however, I think it is only fair that I should present my own credentials. I would never have claimed to have been 'Dylan's best friend', but I think I probably knew him over a longer period of time than any other person in the literary world in which we both moved.

1   Sidney Michaels, *Dylan* (1964)

I am almost certain I first met him towards the end of 1934, on one of my own first visits to London free of parental supervision. The meeting place was the Mitre Coffee House, in Mitre Court, off the south side of Fleet Street, a bit east of Chancery Lane. Our host was Geoffrey Grigson, who was then assistant literary editor of the *Morning Post*, although, owing to the debility of the full editor, he really occupied that position. Neither of us had come to meet Grigson as the emissary of the *Morning Post*. In the important private worlds of each of us, he was simply *New Verse*. The word 'editor' was not needed. Geoffrey was *New Verse* and that was all there was to it.

Dylan, although about four months younger than me, had already reached the peak of achievement for which all young poets at that time aimed. He had been published in *New Verse*. I was not to appear there for another two years, although I have recently learned that Geoffrey, working anonymously, also ran the poetry page of the *Bookman,* where my own first poems appeared—sent there, most kindly, by the editor of *New Verse*.

Dylan, at this time, was short and slim, with lots of curly hair of a neutral brown, and when his full, but not yet blubbery, lips were parted, they disclosed irregular, slightly yellowed, but adequate teeth. A suggestion of the nineties still hung around him. A piece of silk was knotted below a would-be floppy collar and he seemed to be trying to give the impression of a stunted Yeats. To be fair, I was wearing the broadest brimmed black hat Edinburgh could supply, and my own aim was to be Wyndham Lewis as 'The Enemy'[1]. Beside us, Geoffrey must have seemed anonymous.

---

1 Wyndham Lewis's magazine *The Enemy* ran for three issues, 1927-29. It was famed for its biting critical stance.

From then on I saw a considerable amount of Dylan, partly (at the start) because he was a protégé of Norman Cameron[1], with whom I stayed when I moved to London. Norman was some kind of family connection of a sort only known in Scotland; he had been brought up by my grandmother because his own parents were in India.

Over the years, I was cheated by Dylan, bickered with him, drank with him, quarrelled and made it up. He was a friend of a rather difficult sort. I knew that he could and would outsmart me on all occasions, but I also knew he would charm me into forgiving him shortly after. I admired his poetry but I was never certain where I stood with him as a person. I think that he looked upon me, rather improbably, as one of his most reliable friends. This was possibly because I always contrived to have some roof over my head, some room I could call my own.

I know the date of the last time I saw Dylan precisely. It was the 11th of November, 1953. The place was a funeral parlour in New York in the West 60s. Dylan was dead and I had gone up there to see nothing was managed wrongly by Mr McLean, the 'undertaker' as I would have called him, while he, although born in Greenock on the Clyde and still the user of a fine Clydeside accent, preferred the more dismal title of 'mortician'. Everything was in a mess, although a fund and trustees were being set up. I was present as a man of property because my wife owned a house in the Village. This house suggested that—even if we had run out of ready cash two days before because Dylan was an unconscionable time about dying and we had to feed too many vulture

---

1   Norman Cameron (1905-1953) was also a poet. Where mention is made of 'another poet' in 'Laugharne Churchyard in 1954' (p 29), Todd is referring to Norman Cameron's 'A Visit to the Dead'.

mourners—more money would appear when needed.

Having been born in Scotland, I adopted an Edinburgh accent in my dealings with Mr McLean. He was undoubtedly the nicest man of his profession I've ever met. There was no suggestion of 'the Loved One' or even an idea that Dylan might have 'passed over'. Dylan was dead and Mr McLean wanted to know what he was supposed to do about it.

Playing brother-Scots, I managed to choose the cheapest casket in the place. It was cheap by New York standards, although when burying my mother the following year in a Scottish village, I realised its cost would have provided plain pine coffins for all the old ladies within a radius of half a mile. It was covered with a kind of grey baize, stuff that looked and felt as if it had been rejected by the maker of billiard tables and dyed a non-committal battleship color. In addition, it was about the size of a battleship. At a guess I would have said five living Dylans could have squeezed into it and double that number dead could have been crammed inside.

Later, when it was being hoisted ashore by a derrick at Southampton, the mere sight of its bulk nearly caused a heart attack in his old friend Ebby Williams, the landlord of Brown's Hotel in Laugharne, who had driven down in his old Ford hearse to pick it up. It was a tight squeeze, but there was about half an inch clear on each side.

Having succeeded in buying the very cheapest casket Campbells had in stock, Mr McLean realised either that I was not a man of substance or else that I looked at both sides of a nickel before I spent it. He offered, with no suggestion from me, to provide the proper burial clothes from his own little chapel in the Bronx, thereby saving ten dollars. I accepted his offer and he went off for lunch and to collect the garments.

The trouble with its being November 11th was that it was a holiday. Dylan had a perfectly adequate suit, shirt, tie and the rest of it, which would probably have been better buried with him, but all these things were in the care of the New York Police Department and the section dealing with such matters was closed.

I had not seen Dylan since about two days before his death. When I went into the waiting room at St Vincent's Hospital I was surrounded by sobbing and hysterical people of both sexes, and I was being conscientiously and conspicuously tough. I saw no reason for interfering with the balance I had achieved.

The remains now were in a room somewhere off to one side. David Slivka and Ibraim Lassaw were making a death-mask. This was none of my business as I sat in a comfortable chair and read the *Hudson Review*.

When Mr McLean reappeared, he produced the funeral garments. The suit, dark blue, was all right and so was the plain white shirt. The tie, however, stung me, without a thought, to the correct remark, 'My God, Dylan wouldn't be seen dead in *that*.' Mr McLean was not offended, but pointed out that on a holiday shopping was difficult. I went prowling down Broadway and finally found a dark blue bow with white polka dots, already tied. I bought this, returned to the parlour, and gave it to Mr McLean.

I was about to leave when David Slivka, powdered all over with plaster, appeared at my side. Ibraim's wife had called up that Philip Johnson was going to call at the studio, and so Ibraim had rushed away. A visit from Philip Johnson might mean, and this case *did* mean, the sale of a piece of sculpture. David wanted to know whether I could possibly stand the job of helping him remove the carefully segmented pieces of plaster from

Dylan's head.

David told me afterwards I didn't hesitate before going beside him into the room where the corpse was laid out. My own impression was it took me half an hour to decide that—if I didn't keep on thinking of Dylan—it was just another dead body.

The floor was covered with squeezed flat tubes of brushless shaving cream. These had had their contents spread over the face to prevent the plaster sticking. A shapeless form was topped by a huge rough knob of white plaster. I tried to think of other things, such as a beautiful stand of scarlet lobelia I knew on Martha's Vineyard. This didn't work, and I soon realised my thumbs were pushing against a rubbery surface that had once been Dylan. As I helped ease the pieces of plaster off the face, each section was numbered by David and laid carefully in a carton. Piece by piece, the white and lumpy casing disappeared until the whole face was again disclosed, greyish in colour and without any real connection with the man I had had drinks with a week before. Certainly, the face was Dylan's, but it had become completely unreal. That really was the last I saw of my friend, for I had no wish to see him as he was described to me, bedded down in the grey casket with his cheeks rouged and his hair, for some unknown reason, smarmed down and parted somewhere.

I should have decided then that I was done with Dylan. He had been my friend for a long time and we had managed to put up with each other throughout these years. I felt terrible about his death, but that was my own business and I should have retired to lick my wounds in private. I knew it would take a bit of time, but I thought one day I'd get it all out of my mind.

The nagging of memory grew less pernicious during the following three or four years, and I thought there was a good chance of it disappearing completely. Then the Trustees of the Dylan Thomas Estate asked me if I would write the official life, and edit the letters. I might have been able to refuse if Caitlin hadn't thrown her weight into the scales. She said I was the only person she would talk to and the only person she would trust with the letters Dylan had written to her. I tried hard to think of others who could do the job better. Plenty of people had known Dylan in as many (or more) places in England and Wales as I had, but I was the only one who had known him in *some* of these places and who had also known him in some of his American locations. Further, I was on my way to becoming an American citizen and I resented the dishonesty of people such as Kenneth Rexroth using Dylan as a symbol in their declamations against a way of life of which they, personally, disapproved. Honesty had to declare that Dylan died of Dylan. So I accepted the commission.

Maybe it would have been better if the writing of the life had been postponed until Dylan had been dead for fifteen years. It was certainly true that I was the wrong person to have undertaken the assignment so shortly after his death.

I started collecting material in both England and America, and soon began to realise I wasn't collecting material about the odd little Welshman I had known and liked; I was horribly involved in the creation of a mythology. Very few who had known Dylan were able to describe him honestly. Geoffrey Grigson, Bob Pocock and (on the whole) Louis MacNeice refused to subscribe to the hagiography. But there were others— people who had known him for years—who fell into the general mythmaking pattern.

John Davenport, for instance, found himself re- membering occasions upon which he could not possibly have been present. And John was a more than normally intelligent and generally honest man. If someone of *this* intelligence and long standing friendship could go so easily astray, what was I to expect from those of weak intellect and no standing as friends?

It didn't take me long to discover that I had entered a kingdom, or republic, stranger than anything Kafka had imagined. Possibly Nabokov, with a battery of spoofing notes, as in *Pale Fire*, might have been able to cope with the whole affair.

I listened and then went and wrote down what I had heard in notebooks. The notebooks accumulated and I became more and more depressed. When I spread these notebooks around me and tried to get an impression of a single occasion witnessed and reported by, say, six people, I found it was impossible to combine the six to recreate one occasion. I could, I suppose, have ignored the fact that each person had Dylan dressed in a different suit, but I couldn't reconcile the six completely different patterns of behaviour I was supposed to assume had all existed simultaneously. Dylan had ceased to be a real person and had become a figment in the mind of each individual who had met him. Those who had possibly met him two or three times discovered that they had known him from his schooldays, and one 'friend' assured me he had been in St Vincent's Hospital during the whole time of Dylan's dying. He shrugged the matter off as if I was being a tiresome stickler for detail when I pointed out that not only did he not have a passport, but he had, talking about other matters, admitted he had never even crossed the Channel.

As time went by I began to think I was going mad, and I certainly showed some strange symptoms. I hid the notebooks away and—although I added to their number—denied I was making any notes at all. I went around saying, rather grandly, that I was trying to get 'the all-over picture'. I drank too much and found, with a sufficiency of alcohol inside me, I could almost enter into the fantasy of some person I was interviewing.

Not unnaturally, the publishers began to wonder when they were going to get anything at all out of me. I became secretive and elusive. I would not answer letters. I would talk at length about anybody or anything except Dylan. I began to think Sinbad carried a light weight beside my 'old man of the sea'.

All the time, however, I tried to pull myself together by remembering the Dylan whom I had known for nearly twenty years. I compared him with the mythological figures being offered to me, and when one day I found I was beginning to doubt my own memories of Dylan and supplant them with an invention, I decided it was time to give up. I put the notebooks in a closet and left them there, while I tried to get the ghost off my shoulder by doing some serious drinking.

The ghost would not go away, but I got rid of other people's mythologies one day on the beach below the Hotel Formentor during the 1962 Prix Formentor meetings on Mallorca. Sam Lawrence, then with Atlantic Monthly Press, who were to publish the book in America, cornered me. I was both drunk and evasive but when he asked, 'Do you want to give it up? We won't penalize you. Do you want to give up?', I nodded my head dumbly. Sam walked back to the hotel and I lolled on the beach.

The book was taken on by Constantine Fitzgibbon who had the great advantage of never having known Dylan well and of being completely unaware of anything that happened in Wales or England before he himself arrived in Fitzrovia in late 1937. By accepting and rejecting myths on a seemingly whimsical system, he managed to produce something. It wasn't a very accurate account and it was horribly dull, but at least it was a collection of pages. When he came to editing the letters, he had apparently been infected with the myth-making virus, for he supplied notes which were clearly intended to lead the reader into imaginary realms.

Once back in El Terreno (the suburb of Palma where I then lived) I felt better than I had in years. My only trouble was that I had all these notebooks—about thirty-eight of them—filled with several hundred different Dylans. I was still pretty crazy because I found myself pulling them out and picking out a Dylan here and a Dylan there. If I went wrong in my memory of a certain person's myth, I would get out of bed at four in the morning to check and correct myself. I saw I had to get rid of the notebooks. So long as they were in the apartment, I would be haunted.

My craziness came out then. If I had been fully sensible, I would have realised I had written the names of each person interviewed above my section of notes, and that not *all* of them had made myths to involve me. I should have bundled the whole collection up in a carton and put it in store and then have started negotiations with a university about their purchase. But I was in a state of such illogicality that I decided I could only be rid of all my horrible tiny Dylan phantoms by destroying the notebooks in which they were enclosed.

Even more troublesome was the insistence that the books could not, over a period of time, be flushed away down the toilet. They had to be burned. There was no fireplace in my El Terreno apartment, but this may merely have magnified my obsession with the idea that I could only free myself by burning all the evidence. I had plenty of friends with fireplaces, but I had lied myself into a position where I couldn't ask for help.

Perhaps I had hoped that by denying I had any notes, the aspects of Dylan I had recorded would vanish from my mind. But I had been pretty aggressive in my statements about having not yet started to make notes. I had to destroy the notebooks in privacy, and by fire.

Above El Terreno there runs a ridge of hill, topped by Bellver Castle. On all sides there are pinewoods. When not being obsessed, I would walk in the woods and, at the right times of the year, find myself wild-flowers to draw. I found about a dozen different kinds of orchid in the woods and made drawings of seven or eight. Drawing was for a short while my strongest link with sanity. Words were liable to go running off in associations, and sometimes the unconscious would present, like John's head on a salver, a word that (from other associations) hurt even worse. In drawing, with the plant before me, roots, withered leaves and all, I could not wander. The drawings were not botanical drawings as Kew knows them, but private investigations into the private being of an individual plant.

Obviously the burning of the books would have to take place in the Bellver woods. This sounds as if the carrying out of the destruction was a simple job. The woods, being pine, are highly inflammable, and the wandering guardians—fortunately for me few in number—rush to any wisp of smoke they spot. I soon gave up the idea of burning the covers as well as the contents. I cut them up with my pocket-knife and scattered them around. I think it took me nearly a month of early morning walks before I felt every single interview had been charred black and then crumbled to a dust that would be washed away by the next rain.

I knew perfectly well the whole business was merely neurotic nonsense. I had tried to argue myself back into sense and had failed. If pandering to my neuroses helped, I would give them what they sought. At least during the weeks when all my attention was directed toward the burning of the pages, I wasn't troubled by dreams—both sleeping and waking—of hundreds and hundreds of completely unreal Dylans converging on me from all directions.

I dithered my time away in my customary manner, sitting around bars and being brittily witty. In El Terreno, where the drinking part of the Anglo-American colony congregates, a little wit goes a hell of a long way. I was still drinking far too much and suffering from a distrust of written words. Smart rejoinders went out on the air and disappeared, whereas smart remarks in writing would remain as accusers in the sleepless stretches of the night. I had some poems in me, struggling to get out, but I couldn't bring myself to jot them, even in skeleton shape, on the back of an envelope. I could make a limerick or a clerihew, but if someone asked me to write it down, I would escape by explaining I had left my pen at home and I couldn't write with a ballpoint. In drawing rather than writing, I began to think I would be free of my delusions—once I was free of the notebooks.

At this point, with all the notebooks burned, I have no idea what would have happened to me, if I hadn't had the great good fortune to fall in love. I do not know what intuition made her[1] suggest I write my own book on Dylan. I was still nervous about words, but she got me to make a start in December 1963, and, after much rearranging and rewriting, I found, exactly a year later, I had a book of around 90,000 words dealing with Dylan as I had known him, and the world in which we both had moved.

---

1   Todd's friend was an American free-lance editor with whom he began a relationship lasting several years.

I sent copies off to my English and American agents and then I realised I was no longer carrying any image of Dylan around with me.

When Fitzgibbon's non-book, non-biography, appeared early in 1965, I was able to read it with a coldly critical mind. His errors of fact were not parts of a mythology but were merely due to ignorance or laziness. Boy, man and ghost, Dylan had been with me for thirty years and I was glad to be rid of him.

I hastily wrote to my agents and stopped my book going the rounds of publishers. There was no point in publishing it, since it had, with her help and encouragement, finally cleaned my mind of the stupid obsessions which had occupied it for eleven years. All along I had known my fantasies were psychoneurotic, but the recognition had not been strong enough to banish them.

Of course I cannot claim that the vanishing of the mythological Dylan restored me to being the healthy, hard-working and fairly bright person I was up to that day in November, a day which I recall principally because I was the only person close to Dylan who did not break down when his death was announced. I spent the afternoon looking after John Berryman, who was in a state of almost total collapse, and I managed to show no expression of my own feelings. I think one or two people remarked on my callousness, and I rejoiced that they couldn't see behind my facade, a barrier I had been building up ever since I'd been called to the hospital by Liz Reitell and had been forced to play the part of unemotionality.

With St Vincent's Hospital cluttered with the hysterical and prayerful, I had to move as if I had no feelings and no tears to shed. Most of those people who were close to Dylan, and who were in truth his friends, managed to function for a good part of each day. They kept their breakdowns decently private and disappeared from the scene of public wailing. I would not let myself crumble in any way. I was playing the man of iron, and I was always the same at any hour of the day or night.

Now I think I might have been better off if I had joined the clan of moaning nonentities and ninnies. Had I howled in public, like Gene Derwood, or even bayed privately while walking the half-mile or so home from the hospital, I might have been able to cope with all the mixed mythologies I encountered in trying to write the life of Dylan too soon after his death.

Getting rid of the ghost—or whatever it was— took, perhaps, a little longer than I have suggested here. I wasn't free at the moment I finished the book, but on the day I wrote to my agents to stop trying to sell it. I said I wanted to keep it for future use when Dylan would be merely one of a number of friends who had died too soon—Norman Cameron, Louis MacNeice, Bernard Spencer, John Davenport ... no, the list could go on for too long and it would get me nowhere. I had, during the bad years, slipped from being an habitual drinker into becoming an inveterate drunk. I was no longer afraid of words, but I found difficulty in handling them. She, who had started me on my own private book about Dylan, helped me over the drinking piece as well.

When I look at the typescript of my Dylan book, I am ashamed I ever let it go to my agents and glad I called it back. The prose is prose and nothing more. Consistently I used an approximation instead of the *mot juste*. Still I recognise now that the writing of that book, however clumsy, was therapeutic,. If I had not got my own impressions out of my mind, I would now either be dead of drink or still sitting in an El Terreno bar, as unproductive as an egg-bound fowl.

I had not intended to present my credentials at such length or in such depth. It seems a little extravagant to introduce a short and uncharacteristically pleasant aspect of my friend with a long account of how he haunted me after his death. Of course, he encouraged his own legends, for in the nineteen or so years that we knew one another, I can remember how one fantasy might be punctured but there was always another ready to take its place. If I, today, can write about him without creating a different aspect of a too many faceted mythology, it doesn't mean my affection for him has changed. He might have annoyed me to a point where—had I not prided myself upon my self-control—I would happily have beaten him up. He was, in all ways, a superb short-change artist and I was always on the wrong end of the deal. He behaved outrageously to me and my other friends. He was dirty, he pilfered and he lied. But he was, and remains in my memory, my friend. I do not think I can say more than that.

Now, having said all the nasty things about the usual Dylan—the Dylan of the pubs and the clubs, the wide-boy, the smiler with a verbal knife—I think it is only proper that I should give an account of another Dylan. This was a Dylan of whose existence I was unaware. He must have kept it carefully concealed in case his London companions might think he was weakening. After I had recounted this to certain friends, I later found that at least two—men of weak belief—had gone down to question others because they could not accept my unsupported word. I was told they returned to their London haunts wagging wise heads and waiting for some tricky sequel. 'These are they who when the saving thought came shot it for a spy.'[1]

---

1   W H Auden, *The Orators*, 1932.

I WISH I COULD remember how the whole thing started. I had run into Dylan in one of our usual haunts—the Gargoyle Club most likely. Perhaps Dylan had remarked casually that he was fed up with London but didn't want to return to his family in Oxfordshire. It may be that he was having one of his perpetual rows with Caitlin over what she always liked to call 'beastly money'. Whatever the circumstances, I invited Dylan to come down and stay with me in Essex for a couple of days. No sooner had this been accepted, however, than a number of misgivings about the wisdom of my impulsiveness began to creep uneasily through my mind.

In my local village I had set up certain standards of behaviour for myself. Essex villagers are apt to consider anyone from outside, even though it be the next village only a couple miles away, as a 'foreigner.' Acceptance has nothing to do with money, or with the formal respectability of one's normal patterns of behaviour. It depends largely, I think, upon the ability of the foreigner to avoid intruding where he hasn't been invited. As for myself, I believed I had become more or less accepted in Duton Hill. Certainly I drank far too much beer, but I was never the brash outsider who would stride into the local pub calling for drinks all round, expecting to buy friendship with a pint. Naturally such proffered beer would be accepted and drunk, but there would be no warmth to the drinking of it.

As a member of the darts team of the Rising Sun, I played darts for beer. My position as a member of the team was fairly earned in competition with George Hitchin, the captain. Also, I could be expected to take an intelligent interest in agriculture and rural matters. If accidents occurred in the district, such as a cow falling into the ridiculous ditch called the 'Second Line of Defence', I was available to assist and could be relied upon to do what was necessary, without getting in the way.

Looking at Dylan leaning against the bar, clothed in his filmstruck suit, still using some of the wide boy gestures, I wasn't at all sure he would mix with the people of Duton Hill. On the other hand, as I told myself, I had had Lucien Freud and Johnny Craxton down for a weekend and though they certainly had behaved outrageously, it had all been passed off with a 'Got some odd friends, Ruthven, haven't you?'

As soon as we had taken our seats in the first-class compartment of the train at Liverpool Street Station, Dylan became yet another person. The tweeds, which had looked rather horsey and perhaps even a little vulgar in Soho, suddenly changed into the normal attire of a country gentleman. All the way down to Bishop's Stortford, and again in the silly little train that ran to Dunmow, he plied me with questions about the village and the villagers.

A local taxi deposited us at my house and I introduced him to Mrs Ledgerton, my daily (who had come in to set up things for my dinner), and to Fred, the miller, who pumped the water up to my cistern every day. He enchanted them.

When I asked Mrs Ledge, as I called her, about her daughters, for she had only one with her, the other being home with a touch of flu, he was as solicitous as I was myself. He went over to the mill with Fred and watched him set a new ash tooth in the huge wooden wheel which carried the water power to the enormous grinding stones. He ate a good dinner, washed down with Algerian wine, my staple in those days, and accompanied me up to the Rising Sun. There he also captivated George Norris, the licensee, his wife Madge and their daughter, Maureen. He played a reasonable game or two of darts, not winning too often.

Spotting a ring hanging on a rope from the ceiling, he asked me what it was for. 'Ring the Bull,' I told him, and introduced him to the resident expert, a retired farm labourer called Harry Green. Harry explained that the object was to swing the ring on its rope so it would come to rest on a hook on the wall. It sounded terribly easy and, when demonstrated by Harry, looked easy too. I had been taken in that way myself.

Dylan, who on the whole was better at pub games than I was, played several times with Harry. He was defeated every time, if not too badly. Then he challenged me. Although I had been playing the game for a couple of years, he beat me three out of five times. He did not gloat about this. Nor was he bursting with pride when he and I defeated George Norris and George Hitchin at shove-halfpenny. He was, however, largely responsible for the victory.

'We used to play it all the time,' he explained, 'in the Doves and other pubs.' I recalled how Kit Saltmarsh could give either of us several 'beds' and still put us to rout.

We both had a sufficiency of beer and then walked down the hill, taking the short cut between a stream— kingfisher haunted in the sunshine—and a field of tall corn which my landlord, a steel magnate, grew for his prize cattle. Back in the house, we had a final beer and talked of nothing that concerned poetry or the arts, although the walls were lined with books where they weren't covered with drawings and paintings. It was an easy, pleasant evening. When, pretty early on, I suggested bed, he agreed, although there was still plenty of beer in my dairy. This remnant of farming days had huge slate sinks, designed for milk-skimming, but also excellent for keeping things cool.

I was about to give him an Aladdin lamp for his bedside table when he asked if he couldn't have an ordinary lamp. He knew exactly how an Aladdin worked, he claimed, but he also knew it wouldn't work for him. He would be certain, trying to extinguish it, to turn it the wrong way and soot-up both the mantel and the chimney. He was aware of the time and attention it took to burn off a sooted mantel, and also of the risk of breaking the fragile thing.

Next morning I rose before he did. Madge, the post-girl, and Fred—either before or after pumping—would have a cup of tea with me every morning. Hearing the voices, Dylan came down, wrapped in the dressing gown I had dumped in his room the night before. It was much too large for him.

He wanted to know all about Madge's rounds, how she bicycled out around Dunmow every morning and how it was simpler to leave her bike at the Vicarage and walk to my house, across the Abbey Field. There, a ruin—like a Henry Moore sculpture, complete to the hole, marked the Reformation—and there, in the right seasons, I could gather a profusion of ordinary field-mushrooms, horse-mushrooms, blewitts and puffballs. Madge, who always asked after him for the rest of my stay at Tilty, finally had to leave on her appointed rounds.

I made breakfast. Living in the country, I happened (despite rationing) to have plenty of eggs and home-cured bacon. I also had a supply of milk wangled from Ollie Knight, my landlord's herdsman and a famous BBC rural character.

Rather to my surprise, Dylan—whose favourite breakfast I had heard from himself as well as others was kippers and beer—grabbed a pint mug and, pouring for himself from the metal milk-can, drank one pint and then another. We settled down to the bacon and eggs and to enormous cups of tea. I had bought three gargantuan cups in an antique shop in Saffron Walden.

Mrs Ledge, still with only one daughter, had arrived and, telling Dylan that there were ranks of Penguin thrillers on shelves in the hall, I left him in conversation with her.

I retired to my room to work, a long room with windows at either end and with broad, ancient adzed floorboards. I was only interrupted by Mrs Ledge coming in to make my bed, full of praises for my delightful friend.

About midday I went downstairs. The walls of the stairway were curious because I had papered them with the six-inch-to-the-mile Ordnance Survey map of that corner of Essex. Dylan found this fascinating. My outside privy, now used as a garden toolshed, was marked on the map and this intrigued him beyond belief. He insisted that the small black accuracy really showed a dwelling house for tiny people but not, of course, Yeats's 'little people.'

I found him sprawled on the enormous couch. He had a thriller in his hand and a beer in one of my best mugs on the floor beside him. At that time I collected old pub mugs, pink, blue or brown, with glazed tree patterns on the sides. Having discovered my shelves of these, Dylan disdained the ordinary glass pint-mugs of my house and of the London pubs. He laid down his thriller and came with me up to the Rising Sun.

When Jane Lye[1] had left for America, George and Madge Norris had offered to give me lunch with them

1 Todd had been sharing the house with Jane and her children before she left for the USA to join her husband, artist and film maker Len Lye.

every day. In return I gave them my meat rations.
Of course, they could still use those when I was
away, since I then ate in restaurants. I also provided
(another advantage of living in the country) any extra
goodies I happened to lay my sticky hands upon.

The pub hours—different from those of London in
order to fit different patterns of living—were from ten
in the morning until two in the afternoon. As a result
we never ate till after closing time. Now, as if he had
been practising in his sleep, Dylan beat me every time
at Ring the Bull. I took a slight lead on him at darts, but
he then whitewashed me on the slate shove-halfpenny
board.

People from the farms or other local jobs, home for
lunch, dropped in and the conversation was general,
with Dylan taking his proper share but not seeking the
limelight.

I should mention that, as a perpetual user of the
Rising Sun, I ranged from the Saloon Bar to the Public
Bar as I thought fit. George, in horror of mathematics
and in view of my being the possessor of a 'slate' upon
which my bill was jotted down, had long before decided
that, no matter where I was, I should pay one flat
price—the cheaper one.

Lunch, a good hearty stuffed skirt of steak, was most
pleasant, with Dylan flirting reasonably with the ten-
year-old Maureen. Once we had eaten I phoned for a
taxi to come from Great Easton to pick us up early
the following morning, as we both had appointments
in town. Before we left, Dylan thanked Madge for the
lunch (for which she had refused to charge me extra)
and complimented her upon her cooking. So far as
she was concerned he could have stayed in the pub—
although it was closed—drinking beer all afternoon,
but he said he would prefer to return to my house.

We walked down the hill again, spotting a couple of kingfishers by the stream. We gathered an armful of watercress from the ditch. Back in the house Dylan wandered among my books, while I set about making a watercress and potato soup as a part of our evening meal. Then he returned to his thriller while I went back to the one I was writing, which I had promised to churn out by the following day. Owing to Dylan's co-operative behaviour as a guest, it was already nearing completion.

With two breaks only, so far as I remember—one to go down to light the lamps when it became dusk and the other to rescue Dylan when an Aladdin started to smoke up—I worked until I had finished the book.

In the kitchen, which also served as a dining-room for general convenience and for warmth in winter, I set about preparing dinner. It was one of my usual wartime dinners, the watercress and potato soup being followed by an *escalope de Spam*. I did, however, have fresh sweetcorn in the garden, having obtained good seeds from Len Lye in New York. In exchange for some corn, I was given homemade butter by the neighbours. In addition there was the most delicious wholewheat bread. This bread, in little round crusty loaves, was baked in Dunmow by two terribly old sisters, whom Jane's children had a little unkindly christened 'The Witches.' Dylan ate with a good appetite and we shared another bottle of the inevitable Algerian wine, inky stuff though it was.

After that we again returned to the Rising Sun which closed at ten at night. The evening passed much as the previous one had done and just as pleasantly. At closing time George and Madge invited us into the kitchen for a nightcap. They hoped Dylan would return and he said he hoped to do so. I am sure he meant it. Back home we had one beer and went to bed early, conscious of the taxi and the train.

I have, perhaps, extended a day and a half out of all proportion. I had to do so. The Dylan I saw during that brief period was one who was unique to me, relaxed and easy, not trying to be the cynosure but taking his proper place in society. Few of the bits and pieces I have read about him have given even a glimpse of the Dylan I saw then.

In the train, struggling its tired way through suburbs where the Anderson bomb-shelters grew rusty though partly smothered with sweet peas and scarlet runners, I realised two things. The first was that I had never, not even in the early British Grove days, spent so long a time alone with Dylan—alone, that is, except for people who were strangers. The second was that—although there had been ample opportunity for such discussions—we had not talked about poetry or literature.

These two days remain fresh in my memory and I do not think there is one single rough edge for that memory to wish to file smooth. Were this the only Dylan I have had to recall, I would not have been haunted so for those last years.

Ruthven Todd:

LAUGHARNE CHURCHYARD IN 1954

Three thousand miles and nearly half a year
Away from a drab November afternoon; hysterics
Of friends forgotten, and also the plain derricks
Hoisting the grey coffin, I myself stand here

Savouring the early spring and Camarthen mist,
Looking at humped soil and at the celandine
That grows on turned earth, flourishing between
Knotgrass and coltsfoot which the digger missed

While breaking clods. By the old stone wall
The primroses are showing, and on mud flats
The heron calls; the sea comes in, and rats
Gnaw at gifts the estuary brings them all.

This morning I walked with the gold-polled son
In search of imaginary cows, while bluebells
And violets distracted us, but all their smells
Were redolent of hospital. Suddenly I was one

Who thought of the death of him, my friend,
In a far country where he was a stranger, while
I knew it now as home. The child's bright smile
Reflected the father's face, the path would wend

Across his landscape, and the lonely crying birds
Yammered his background. Now, in this untidy
Churchyard, looking at sodden soil, I recall the mighty
Swell of that voice, the roll and thunder of words

In public places, but, more particularly, the bars
And friendly houses where we would meet and joke
About our situation, we, the perennially broke,
With, always, limericks and gossip about the stars

Of our own worlds, those whom success had loved.
Now, past the thin iron gates, past the wall-rue
And hart's-tongue, success, my friend, has taken you
To that country which another poet had already proved

A source for fabulous tales. Damp now, I shiver,
Take a last look at the awkward hump of earth,
Recalling that your funeral gave rise to mirth,
And turn away, knowing certainly that I will never

Again stand thus. Time and fame will neatly trim
This rubbish heap, and this grave itself become
A symbol of the poet in his long-sought home.
And I, forgetting this, carry my memories of him,

My jester, drinking companion, and old friend,
Sharer of careless youth and slapdash middle age.
Records preserve his voice, his words are on the page
To prove that this drear mistiness is not the end.

AFTERWORD

THE POET, NOVELIST and William Blake scholar Ruthven Todd[1] was born in Edinburgh in 1914, and so shares his centenary with Dylan Thomas. They did not meet until 1934, but thereafter they saw much of each other in London, where they roistered together, stole each other's girlfriends, composed scurrilous verse and, strictly in the spirit of research, demonstrated it was possible to drink in licensed premises for a continuous 24-hour period. They shared a liking for the hard-boiled detective fiction emerging for the first time in American magazines, and were to be found at the docks whenever a ship from the US arrived, rooting through bundles of discarded magazines used as ballast, looking for copies of *Black Mask*. During Dylan's four trips to America between 1950 and 1953 they met up often in New York's Greenwich Village where Dylan made final revisions to the manuscript of *Under Milk Wood* in the basement of Ruthven's house.

Their personalities differed: Ruthven had an essential innocence, generosity and openness of personality which endeared him to most people. Dylan was pretty much the opposite: many who met him didn't like him much, including Ruthven's first wife. Nevertheless, the two men formed a bond, and Ruthven knew Dylan at least as well, and over a longer period, as most outside Dylan's immediate family—a fact Dylan's biographers have largely failed to appreciate. This is probably because a primary source for biography lies in written correspondence, and little, if any, of this exists between Ruthven and Dylan. Dylan's widow Caitlin, however, knew how close their friendship was. This is why she

---

1 'Ruthven' derives from the Gaelic *Ruadhainn* and is pronounced 'riven'.

chose Ruthven to write Dylan's official biography, although (for reasons explained in his memoir) Ruthven was never the right person to do it. Ruthven's name is mainly recorded in association with Dylan because of the important role he played in the theatrical events surrounding Dylan's death. These events are recorded in painful detail in an eleven-page letter Ruthven wrote to Louis MacNeice, the text of which can be accessed on the official Dylan Thomas website.

Ruthven was not adept or comfortable expressing personal feeling in his prose writings, but I think he achieved this in 'Laugharne Churchyard in 1954', which he drafted during a visit to Wales to see Dylan's family and his grave, completing it in America the following year. For me, it is among the best of his poems. Although I never met Ruthven in person, I do at least know what he sounded like. I am lucky to have a digital copy of a scratchy recording from 1955 where he recites 'Laugharne Churchyard in 1954' in a rather BBC-style accent that betrays little trace of his Edinburgh upbringing. When he reaches the end of the poem, there's a short pause before he asks: 'Is that enough?'

Peter Main, February 2014.